Florida

142 PICTURES
SCENES OF PARADISE

Photos Copyright 1991 by Werner J. Bertsch
Text by Aida Corrada-Bertsch
Design by Werner J. Bertsch
© 1991 by Werner J. Bertsch

Softcover I.S.B.N. 1-877833-06-1/Hardcover I.S.B.N. 1-877833-07-X
Published by
Pro Publishing Inc.
P.O. Box 350335
Fort Lauderdale, Florida 33335, USA
Printed in Italy by Kina Italia, Milan, Italy

There has been life in Florida for millions of years. Fossils of amphibious creatures have been found, dated from 120 million years ago. Geologists agree that groups of Asians looking for a warmer climate and fertile land, crossed a land bridge linking Siberia to Alaska 20,000 years ago. They made their way down to Canada and the continental U.S. and about 10,000 years ago reached the Florida Panhandle.

The European who is given credit for discovering Florida is Spain's Don Juan Ponce de Leon. After 25 days of sailing in the Bahamas, the crew celebrated "Pascua Florida", the Feast of Flowers or Easter, on board the ships "Santa Maria de la Consolacion" and the "Santiago". Six days later, on April 2, 1513, they discovered a new land and named it "La Florida." Upon arrival in this new land, the Spanish encountered unfriendly natives named "Calusas" or "Mayaimas", who attacked with an unrelenting furry of arrows and stones. Battles between the native people and Spaniards continued for years.

In the 16th century, French, Dutch and English pirates attacked the Spanish ships which were full of booty- "pieces of eight", gold and silver. Many times these captured treasures were buried on the Florida beaches. Other times hurricanes sank the treasure filled ships off the coasts.

In 1763 in the First Treaty of Paris, the Spaniards gave control of Florida to England in exchange for Havana. While England was preoccupied with fighting the Americans in 1776, Spain took advantage and recaptured all of Western Florida. The Second Treaty of Paris was signed in 1783 and gave Florida back to Spanish rule. Spain sold Florida in 1821 to the United States in exchange for five million in debts. A village of the Talasi Indians became the state capital, named Tallahassee in 1823.

By then Oconee Creeks had migrated from Georgia to Florida and became known as Se-mi-no-lee meaning "wild ones" or "runaways" in the Creek language. Three wars were fought trying to move these people by force to reservations in the Arkansas Territory. A group of about 300 remained uncaptured and retreated far into the sawgrass rivers of the Everglades. They are the ancestors of the present day Seminole and Miccosukee Tribes living in the Everglades.

Florida became a state in March 3, 1845. Later Florida sided with the other Confederate States and seceded from the Union on January 10, 1861. The plantation owners did not want to give up their slaves, and so Florida entered the Civil War. The North won and the American flag flew over Tallahassee again on May 30, 1865.

In the early 1920's Henry Morrison Flagler built the East-coast Railroad extending to Palm Beach; and Henry Plant built the Atlantic Coastline Railroad from Virginia to Tampa. Many extravagant hotels were built along the stops to attract visitors to this magical land. Julia D. Tuttle convinced Flagler to extend the railroad to Biscayne Bay in 1896, and Miami was born. The tracks went to Homestead in 1903 and to Key West in 1912. So, Florida became linked to the rest of the nation, and visitors came by the train-load. This was the start of Florida as the "Vacation Land."

Today, Florida is one of the fastest growing states with visitors from all over the world. The sandy beaches and the warm climate provide visitors with a variety of recreational and relaxing activities. Florida has 1,300 miles of shoreline, 800 of those being beaches. Yet it is also one of the largest producers of dairy products and citrus fruits in the U.S.A..

Florida will remain America's number one vacation destination, because of all the modern changes that have enhanced the charm and flavor of this "Tropical Paradise." From history, water sports to restaurants and night-life, it can all be found in "Glorious Florida."

Wie Fossilienfunde beweisen, hat schon vor 120 Mill Jahren Leben in Florida existiert.

Geologen haben erforscht, daß for ungefähr 20.000 ren ein asiatisches Volk auf der Suche nach fruchtb Land eine Landbrücke zwischen Asien und Alaska querte und nach weiteren 10.000 Jahren Florida errei Der spanische Seefahrer Don Juan Ponce de Leon deckte Florida. Nach 25 Tagen auf See feierte Manschaft auf den Bahamas das Fest "Pascua Flor das "Fest der Blumen" oder auch Osterfest. Am 12 1513, genau 6 Tage später, entdeckten die Schiffe "S Maria de la Consolacion" und "Santiago" neues L welches sie "La Florida" nannten.

Jahrzehntelang kämpften die Eingeborenen Stämme Calusas" oder auch die "Mayaimas", erbittert geger spanische Besetzung.

Französische, holländische und englischen Piraten kierten im 16. Jahrhundert die mit Gold und Edelste reich beladenen spanischen Schiffe. Viele der Sch sind in Florida vergraben, einige wurden durch s Stürme auch in die See versenkt.

Florida fiel, durch den Pariser Vertrag, im Jahre 176 die Engländer, welche den Spaniern dafür Havar Kuba überließen. Den Kampfschwerpunkt zu dieser richteten die Engländer aber gegen die Amerikaner, so eroberten die Spanier den westlichen Teil Florida Jahre 1776 zurück. Schon 1783 wurde im zweiten Pa Vertrag Florida wieder den Spaniern zugesprochen, che aber das Land gegen 5 Millionen Dollar im Jahre an die Amerikaner verkauften. Ein kleines Indianerdor dem Namen "Talasi" wurde zur Hauptstadt erkoren, später, nämlich 1823, auf den Namen Tallahassee ur nannt.

Zu dieser Zeit wanderten südlich von Georgia die Oco Creek Indianer nach Florida. Man nannte sie einfach "Wilden" oder auch Se-mi-no-lee. Nach drei Krie wurden die Indianer in ein Reservat in Arkansas umg delt. 300 Indianer konnten jedoch entkommen und fl teten in die Everglades, wo sie die beiden Stämme M sukee und Seminole gründeten.

Am 3. März 1845 wurde Florida offiziell ein Staat der L Im Bürgerkrieg zwischen den Nord und Südstaaten tr te sich Florida allerdings von den USA um auf der S der Südstaaten zu kämpfen, um die Sklaverei auf Plantagen aufrechterhalten zu können. Da die Nords ten den Krieg aber gewannen, wurde am 3. Mai 1865 amerikanische Flagge in Tallahassee wieder gehißt.

Henry Morrison Flagler erbaute in den 20er Jahren die Jahrhunderts die Ostküsteneisenbahnlinie bis nach F Beach, und Henry Plant die Verbindung von Virginia r Jacksonville.

Eine Vielzahl von Hotels wurde entlang der Eisenbah richtet. Julia D. Tuttle überzeugte Flagler von der Idee Bahnlinie bis zur Biscayne Bucht zu verlängern. Dies die Geburt von Miami. Die Eisenbahnlinie wurde dan Jahre 1903 bis Homestead erweitert und erreichte West im Jahre 1912.

Damit war Florida von überall leicht erreichbar, und Besucherstrom nahm zu.

Das war dann auch der Start für das Ferienland Flor welches heute zu den Staaten mit den größten Zuwa raten zählt und Erhohlungssuchende aus der ganzen V beherbergt. Strände, die mehr als 1330 km lang sind das warme Klima bieten ideale Voraussetzungen für e Urlaub.

Die Städte haben sich in den vergangen Jahren drast verändert und moderne Architektur bestimmt den Bau Trotz allem wird Florida als Urlaubsland die "Num Eins" bleiben, denn alle diese Neuerungen haben Charme dieses tropischen Paradieses noch verbessert

En la Florida ha existido vida por millones de años. Fósiles anfibios de animales se han encontrado de 120 millones de años. Los Geólogos están de acuerdo en que grupos de Asiáticos buscando un clima caluroso y tierra fértil cruzaron un puente de tierra conectando Siberia a Alaska hace 20,000 años. Ellos cruzaron Canadá y el resto del continente de los Estados Unidos, y llegaron al norte de la Florida hace 10,000 años.

Don Juan Ponce de León fue el Español que mereció el crédito por descubrir la Florida. Después de 25 días navegando las Bahamas, los marineros celebraron la Pascua Florida en los barcos "Santa Maria de la Consolación" y el "Santiago". Seis días después el 2 de Abril de 1513, descubrieron un nuevo territorio y lo llamaron "La Florida". Cuando llegaron los Españoles se encontraron con indígenas llamados "Calusas" o "Mayaimas". Los cuales atacaron con flechas y piedras. Las guerras continuaron entre los indígenas y los Españoles por muchos años.

En el siglo 16, piratas Franceses, Hollandeses e Ingleses atacaban los barcos Españoles llenos de monedas, oro y plata. Muchas veces estos tesoros fueron enterrados en las playas Floridanas. Otras veces los uracanes hundían los barcos llenos de tesoros en las costas.

En 1763 en el Primer Tratado de Paris, los Españoles le dieron control de la Florida a Inglaterra en cambio por la Habana. Mientras que Inglaterra estaba ocupada en guerra con los Americanos en 1776, España recapturó todo el este de la Florida. El Segundo Tratado de Paris fue firmado en 1783 y le dió control de la Florida a los Españoles. España vendió la Florida a los Estados Unidos por cinco millones en deudas. La aldea de Indios Talasi se convertió en la capital estatal en 1823, llamada Tallahassee.

En este tiempo los indios Oconee Creeks emigraron desde Georgia a la Florida y fueron reconocidos por Semi-no-lee que significa "salvajes" o "fugitivos" en el idioma Creek. Tres guerras fueron peleadas tratando de mandar a los Indios a reservaciones en el Territorio de Arkansas. Un grupo de 300 se escondieron en los ríos y malezas en los Everglades. Ellos son los antepasados de las tribus de Seminoles y Miccosukee de hoy.

La Florida se convertió en estado en Marzo 3 de 1845. Luego tomo el partido con el resto de los Estados Confederados y se separó del resto de la Unión en Enero 10 de 1861. Los dueños de plantaciones no querian liberar a los esclavos y la Florida entró en la Guerra Civil. El Norte ganó la guerra y la bandera Americana hondeó sobre Tallahasse otra vez en Mayo 30 de 1865.

En la primera parte del siglo 20, Henry Morrison Flagler construyó el Ferrocarril Eastcoast extendiendose hasta Palm Beach, y Henry Plant construyó el Ferrocarril Atlantic Coastline desde Virginia hasta Tampa. Muchos hoteles lujosos fueron construidos en las paradas para atraer a los visitantes a esta tierra mágica. Julia D. Tuttle convenció a Flagler que extendiera el ferrocarril hasta la Bahía Biscayne en 1896, y nació Miami. La vía fue extendida hasta Homestead en 1903 y a Cayo Hueso en 1912. Entonces la Florida se unió al resto de la nación, y los trenes venian llenos de visitantes. Ésto fue el comienzo de la Florida como "Lugar de Vacaciones".

Hoy la Florida es uno de los estados de más crecimiento, con visitantes desde todas las partes del mundo. Las playas y el clima caluroso les dan a los visitantes una variedad de actividades recreacionales. La Florida tiene 1,300 millas de costas y 800 millas de playas. También es reconocido como uno de los estados de producción de productos lácteos y frutas cítricas de los Estados Unidos.

La Florida seguirá siendo el número uno para vacaciones, por todos los cambios modernos que la han convertido en un "Paraíso Tropical". Desde historia, deportes, restaurantes, y vida nocturna, todo se puede encontrar en "La Florida Gloriosa".

Des fossiles de créatures amphibies ont été découverts, datant de 120 millions d'années. Des géologues reconnaissent que des groupes d'Asiatiques recherchant un climat plus chaud et une terre fertile, ont traversé un pont terrestre reliant le Sibérie à l'Alaska il y a 20,000 ans. Ils traversèrent le Canada et les Etats-Unis et atteignirent les nord-ouest de la Floride il y a 10,000 ans environ.

L'européen qui est reconnu pour avoir découvert la Floride est Don Juan Ponce de Leon d'Espagne. Après 25 jours de navigation dans les Bahamas, l'équipage a célébré la "Pascua Florida", la Fête des Fleurs ou Pâques, à bord des navires "Santa Maria de la Consolación" et "Santiago". Six jours plus tard, le 2 avril 1513, ils découvrirent une nouvelle terre et l'appelèrent "La Floride". Lors de l'arrivée dans cette nouvelle terre, les Espagnols rencontrèrent des indigènes hostiles appelés les "Calusas" ou "Mayaimas", qui attaquèrent avec une fureur implacable avec des flèches et des pierres. Des batailles entre les indigènes et les Espagnols continuèrent pendant des années.

Au 16ème siècle des pirates français, hollandais et anglais attaquèrent les navires espagnols qui étaient pleins de butin, de doublons espagnols, d'or et d'argent. Souvent ces trésors capturés étaient enterrés sur les plages de Floride. Dans d'autres cas, des ouragans ont provoqué des naufrages de navires remplis de trésors au large des côtes.

En 1763, lors du premier traité de Paris, les Espagnols cédèrent la Floride à l'Angleterre en échange de La Havane. Tandis que l'Angleterre était préoccupée à lutter contre les Américains en 1776, l'Espagne en profita et recaptura toute la Floride occidentale. Le second traité de Paris fut singé en 1783 et rendit la Floride à l'autorité de l'Espagne. L'Espagne vendit la Floride en 1821 aux Etats-Unis en échange de cinq millions de dollars de dettes. Un village d'Indiens Talasi devint la capitale de l'état, appelée Tallahassee en 1823.

Entretemps les Indiens Oconee Creeks avaient fait migration de Géorgie en Floride et furent connus sous le nom de Semi-mi-no-lee voulant dire "les sauvages" ou "les fuyards" en langue Creek. Trois guerres ont eu lieu pour essayer de déplacer ces peuplades par la force dans des réserves situées dans le territoire de l'Arkansas. Un groupe de 300 environ ne furent pas capturés et retraitèrent loin dans les cours d'eau des Everglades remplis de souchets à dents de scie. Ce sont les ancêtres des tribus de Séminoles et de Miccosukee d'aujourd'hui vivant dans les Everglades.

La Floride est devenue un état le 3 mars 1845. Plus tard la Floride pris le parti des autres Etats confédérés et fit sécession de l'Union le 10 janvier 1861. Les propriétaires de plantation ne voulurent pas renoncer à leurs esclaves, et c'est ainsi que la Floride participa à la Guerre Civile. Le Nord gagna et le drapeau américain flotta à nouveau sur Talahassee le 30 mai 1865. Au début du 20ème siècle, Henry Morrison Flagler construisit le chemin de fer Eastcoast Railroad s'étendant jusqu'à Palm Beach; et Henry Plant construisit le chemin de fer Atlantic Coastline Railroad de la Virginie à Tampa. Un grand nombre d'hôtels extravagants ont été construits tout au long des arrêts pour attirer les visiteurs dans ce pays magique. Julia D. Tuttle réussit à convaincre Flagler de prolonger le chemin de fer jusqu'à la baie de Biscayne en 1896, et Miami était né. Les voies allèrent jusqu'à Homestead en 1903 et à Key West en 1912. De sorte que la Floride fut reliée au reste du pays, et les visiteurs arrivèrent par trains complets. C'était le début de la Floride en tant que "Terre des vacances".

Aujourd'hui, la Floride est l'un des états dont la croissance est la plus rapide avec des visiteurs venant de tous les coins du monde. Les plages de sable et le climat chaud apportent aux visiteurs une variété de distractions et de possibilités de détente. La Floride a une côte de 2,092 kilomètres, dont près de 1,300 sont des plages. Toutefois, elle est aussi un des plus importants producteurs de produits laitiers et d'agrumes des Etats-Unis.

La Floride restera la destination de vacances numéro un de l'Amerique, en raison de tous les changements modernes qui sont mis en vedette par le charme et l'arôme de ce "paradis tropical". Depuis les sports nautiques aux restaurants et aux activités nocturnes, on trouve tous dans la merveilleuse Floride.

Photo page 1: Flamingo at Metro Zoo, Miami
Page 4/5: Key West

Key West is the southernmost city of the continental United States. Built on centuries of rich history, it features the famous sunset on Mallory Square, the Ernest Hemingway Home and Museum, the Southernmost Point, and Tennessee Williams Home. Take a ride on the Trolley or Conch Train, to discover this Buccaneer Village.

Key West ist die südlichst gelegene Stadt Amerikas und wurde vor Jahrhunderten von Seeräubern gegründet. Der berühmte Sonnenuntergang am Mallory Square, die Häuser von Ernest Hemingway und Tennessee Williams sind nur einige der wichtigsten Anziehungspunkte. Erleben Sie die unvergleichliche Atmosphäre dieser Stadt bei einer Rundfahrt mit dem Conch Train oder dem Trolley.

La punta más al sur del continente de los Estados Unidos es Cayo Hueso. Está construido sobre cientos de años de rica historia, y el Mallory Square, la Casa y Museo de Ernest Hemingway, el Punto Sur, el Tren Concha y la casa de Tennessee Williams se encuentran aquí.

Key West est la ville la plus au sud des Etats-Unis. Erigée sur des siècles remplis d'histoire, elle se distingue par le fameux coucher de soleil sur le square Mallory, la maison et le musée d'Ernest Hemingway, et la maison de Tennessee Williams. Faites un tour avec le tramway ou le Conch Train pour découvrir ce Village des boucaniers.

Top: Key West, Duval Street
Right: Ernest Hemingway Home and Museum
Page 7 Top: Key West Beach
Bottom left: Key West Lighthouse
Bottom right: Key West Conch House

6

Top Panorama: Florida Keys, Conch Key
Left: Fishing boats at sunset
Right: Bahia Honda State Park
Page 10/11: 7 Mile Bridge

The Florida Keys are a chain of islands expanding southwest into the Gulf of Mexico. Some of the major attractions are: Theater of the Sea, Seven Mile Bridge, Bahia Honda State Park. In John Pennekamp State Park, scuba and snorkeling trips to the reefs are available.

Die Florida Keys sind eine Inselkette im Golf von Mexico, dem Festlande vorgelagert. Einige der Hauptattraktionen sind das "Theater of thea Sea", die "Sieben Meilen Brücke", die "Bahia Honda Brücke mit Park". Der "John F. Pennekamp Park" ist der ideale Ausgangspunkt für Schnorchel- und Tauchausflüge zu den Korallenriffen südlich des Parks.

Los Cayos Floridanos son una cadena de islas extendiéndose suroeste en el Golfo de Méjico. Algunas de las atracciones son el Teatro del Mar, el Puente de Las Siete Millas y de Bahía Honda, con el parque estatal, y el Parque Pennekamp donde se puede ir de scuba a los arrecifes.

Les cayes de Floride sont une chaine d'îlots à fleur d'eau s'étendant vers le sud-ouest dans le Golfe du Mexique. Un certain nombre des principales attractions sont: le théâtre de la mer, le pont de sept milles, le parc d'état de Bahia Honda. On peut effectuer des excursions de plongée sous-marine et de schnorchel dans les récifs du parc John Pennekamp.

Opposite page: John Pennekamp State Park, school of Grunts
Photo by Larry Lipsky
Top left: Theater of the Sea, Islamorada
Bottom left: Marathon Lighthouse
Right: Sandy Beach, Plantation
Page 14/15: Key Biscayne, Miami

Miami is a truly Metropolitan City, with the largest cruise-port in the United States. Modern architecture is combined with Mediterranean and European styles, giving Miami a unique appearance. Parrot Jungle, Vizcaya Museum, Seaquarium, Bayside Marketplace are just a few of the major attractions. Metromover and Metrorail provide all necessary transportation around the city.

Miami ist eine der modernsten Städte Amerikas und besitzt den größten Kreuzfahrthafen der Welt. Die zeitgemäße Architektur ist vermischt mit europäischem und spanischem Stil.
Der "Parrot Jungle", das "Vizcaya Museum", das "Seaquarium" und "Bayside Marketplace" sind nur einige der vielen Sehenswürdigkeiten. Mit dem Metromover und dem Metrorail kommen sie rasch von einer Attraktion zur nächsten.

Miami es una ciudad metropolitana, con el puerto para barcos cruceros más grande de U.S.A.. La arquitectura moderna es combinada con influencias Mediterráneas y Europeas. Algunas de las atracciones son, La Jungla de los Papagayos, el Museo Vizcaya, Seaquarium, y el Mercado Bayside. Metromover y Metrorail proporcionan toda la transportación necesaria alrededor de la ciudad.

Miami est réellement une ville métropolitaine, avec le plus grand port de croisières des Etats-Unis. L'architecture moderne se combine aux styles méditerranéen et européen, donnant à Miami un aspect unique en son genre. La jungle des perroquets, le musée Vizcaya, le Seaquarium, la jungle des singes, la place du marché au bord de la baie, sont juste quelques unes des principales attractions. Metromover et Metrorail apportent tout ce qu'il faut en matière de transport en commun dans toute l'agglomération urbaine.

Top: Miami Skyline with Cruise Ships
Right: Fisher Island with Miami in the background
Page 17 left: Biscayne Blvd with Metro Mover
Page 17 from top to bottom: Villa Vizcaya, Miami
Skyline at sunset, Parrot Jungle and Gardens, Miami Seaquarium

Miami Seaquarium

In Hollywood, visitors enjoy restaurants, shops, and hotels directly on the Atlantic Ocean. Fort Lauderdale called "America's Venice," has luxurious homes bordering the many canals. Fishing on the Deerfield Beach Pier or just relaxing in the sun in Delray and in Lake Worth is a "visitors dream come true."

Genießen Sie den wundervollen Strand von Hollywood mit all seinen Restaurants und Geschäften. Wegen der vielen Wasserkanäle wird Fort Lauderdale auch das "Venedig Amerikas" genannt. Entlang der besagten Wasserwege stehen wuderschöne Häuser und Villen. Hier können Sie Ihre Urlaubsträume in Realität verwandeln, indem Sie z. B. am Deerfield Beach Pier fischen oder einfach auspannen und nichts tun.

Top: Fort Lauderdale Beach
Bottom left: Deerfield Beach
Bottom right: Fort Lauderdale Waterways

En Hollywood los visitantes disfrutan de restaurantes, tiendas y hoteles directamente en el Mar Atlántico. Fort Lauderdale es llamado "La Venecia de América", con casas lujosas bordeando los canales. Pescando en el muelle de Deerfield o solamente descansando en el sol en Delray y Lake Worth son un "Sueño Convertido en Realidad" para los vacacionistas.

ywood les visiteurs trouvent des restaurants, des
ues et des hôtels sur la plage. Fort Lauderdale appelé
nise de l'Amérique'', a des villas luxueuses le long
mbreux canaux. Pêcher sur le ponton de Deerfield
ou simplement se reposer au soleil à Delray et au
Vorth c'est vraiment le "rêve devenu réalité" du

Pompano Beach and Boca Raton are elegant vacation destinations. Many shopping areas, famous resorts and hotels are located here.

Pompano Beach und Boca Raton gehören zu den eleganteren Urlaubszielen. Viele Einkaufszentren und berühmte Hotels machen Ihren Urlaub unvergeßlich.

Top: Pompano Beach
Middle: Intracoastal Waterway in Pompano Beach
Below: Lantana
Opposite page: Boca Raton Hotel and Club

Pompano Beach y Boca Ratón son unas comunidades muy elegantes. Muchas áreas de compras, y famosos hoteles están localizados aquí.

Pompano Beach et Boca Raton sont d'élégantes destinations de vacances. On y trouve de nombreux quartiers de magasins, des villégiatures et des hôtels en renom.

Opposite page: Eastcoast Sunrise
Top: Lake Worth
Left: West Palm Beach
Below: West Palm Beach, Downtown
Page 28/29: Palm Beach

Palm Beach is known for the winter homes of millionaires. Worth Avenue is considered one of the most exclusive shopping streets in the world.

Amerikas Millionäre haben Palm Beach als Winterdomizil entdeckt. So kommt es auch, daß eine der teuersten Einkaufstraßen hier zu finden ist: Worth Avenue.

Palm Beach es llamada la casa de invierno de los millonarios. Worth Avenue es considerada como una de las calles mas exclusivas para compras en el mundo.

Top right: Palm Beach
Top left: Worth Avenue, Palm Beach
Bottom left: Poinciana Mall, Palm Beach
Below right: Breakers Hotel, Palm Beach
Opposite page top: Jupiter Lighthouse
Bottom: Riviera Beach

Palm Beach est connu pour ses villas d'hiver de millionnaires. Worth Avenue est considérée comme une des rues commerçantes les plus élégantes du monde.

OSCEOLA'S
INDIAN VILLAGE
SOUVENIR SHOP & ALLIGATORS

Le Parc national des Everglades est l'un des plus grands parcs protégés des Etats-Unis. C'est le foyer des Indiens Séminoles et Miccosukee. Il y a une grande variété de faune; le plus fameux est l'alligator. Des excursions en aéroglisseur font participer les visiteurs à une merveilleuse aventure à travers les Everglades.

Preceding page top: Everglades Airboat rides
Bottom: Osceola's Indian Village, Everglades
This page top: Alligators
Middle: Miccosukee Indian Family
Left: Seminole Indian
Opposite page top: Loxahatchee National Wildlife Refuge
Middle left: Anhinga
Middle right: White Herons
Bottom: Sunset in the Everglades

The Everglades National Park is one of the largest protected parks in the United States. It is home to the Seminole and Miccosukee Indians. A great variety of wildlife abounds; the most famous is the alligator. Rides on airboats take visitors on a wonderful adventure across the Everglades.

Der Everglades National Park gehört zu den größten Nationalparks Amerikas. Die Seminole und Miccosukee Indianer leben in dieser sumpfartigen Gegend. Für viele exotische Tierarten ist dieser Nationalpark die Lebensgrundlage; zu den berühmtesten zählt sicherlich der Florida-Aligator. Eine Fahrt mit dem Propellerboot wird für Sie bestimmt ein unvergeßliches Erlebnis sein.

El Parque Everglades es uno de los parques más grandes de los Estados Unidos. Las tribus de Indios Seminoles Y Miccosukee hacen sus casa en el pantano, también es habitada por una gran cantidad de pájaros y animales y el más famoso es el caimán. Viajes en los "barcos de aire" or airboats llevan a los visitantes en una aventura maravillosa alrededor de los Everglades.

Naples' spectacular "sunset at the pier" attracts visitors as well as native Floridians daily. Olde Naples is a beautiful shopping area, and fine residential communities are in walking distance. Miles of white beaches provide Marco Island with a peaceful surrounding.

Einer der spektakulären Sonnenuntergänge finden Sie am Pier von Naples. Etliche Touristen und Einwohner bewundern dieses einzigartige Naturschauspiel gleichermaßen. Aber auch einkaufen wird hier zur Erholung, und zwar in "Olde Naples", einem wunderschönen Einkaufsviertel. Hier befindet sich ebenfalls eine der besten Wohngegenden Floridas. Südlich von Naples liegt Marco Island, eine Insel mit langen sandstränden und viel Ruhe zur Erholung!

La puesta del sol en el muelle de Naples es espectacular, atrayendo a visitantes a igual que a nativos Floridanos diariamente. Olde Naples es una zona de compras bellisima y la comunidad de lujosas casas están cerca. Millas de playas blancas proporcionan a Marco Island tranquilidad.

Le spectaculaire "coucher de soleil sur le quai" à Naples attire tous les jours les visiteurs aussi bien que les Floridiens natifs. Old Naples est rempli de superbes magasins et des quartiers résidentiels sont faciles à atteindre à pied. Des kilomètres de plages blanches font de Marco Island un environnement paisible.

Sanibel and Captiva islands are the tropical paradise of Fort Myers, with a Caribbean flavor. In Fort Myers the Thomas Edison Winter Home is located.

Die Sanibel und Captiva Inseln sind die tropischen Paradiese von Fort Myers.
Sie haben das Flair der Karibik und sind wegen der vielen Muscheln am Strand sehr beliebt und berühmt.
In Fort Myers finden Sie auch das Haus und Labor des Erfinders Thomas Edison.

Opposite page: Everglades National Park
This page top: Fort Myers
Middle: Sunset at the beach
Bottom right: Thomas Edison, Winter
Home and Museum
Bottom: Fort Myers Downtown

Las islas Sanibel y Captiva son el paraíso de Fort
Myers, con un sabor Caribeño. En Fort Myers la
Casa y Museo de Thomas Edison está localizada.

Les îles Sanibel et Captiva sont le paradis tropical
de Fort Myers. Elles capturent l'ambiance des
Caraïbes. C'est là que se trouve la maison d'hiver
de Thomas Edison.

Below: Shells at Sanibel Is
Bottom: Aerial view of Sanibel Is
Bottom left: Captiva Is
Opposite Page: Captiva Is
Following page 42/43: John Ringling Muse
Art Museum of Flo

Opposite page top: Boca Grande
Bottom left: St. Armands Circle, Sarasota
Bottom right: Punta Gorda
This page bottom: Anna Maria Island
Right: Sarasota Bay

St. Petersburg is located on the southern tip of the Pinellas peninsula. Clearwater is nicknamed "The Sparkling City." For water-sports, relaxation, and silver sands, it can not be beat.

St. Peterburg liegt am südlichen teil der Pinellas Halbinsel. An der Sonnenküste liegt die "funkelnde Stadt" - Clearwater. Das Angebot an Wassersport und Enspannungsmöglichkeiten am Silbersandstrand ist schier unschlagbar.

St. Petersburg está localizado en la punta sur de la Península Pinellas. Clearwater es nombrada "La Ciudad Brillante". Para deportes marítimos, descansar y por las arenas plateadas no tienen competencia.

St-Petersburg est situé à la pointe méridionale de la péninsule Pinellas. Clearwater est surnommée "La ville pétillante". Il n'y a pas sa pareille pour les sports nautiques, la détente et les sables argentés.

Top: Clearwater Beach
Middle: Beach scene
Bottom: Sunset in Clearwater
Opposite page: Tarpon Springs
Following pages 50/51: Tampa at night
Page 52/53: Orlando at twilight

Yearly millions of people visit the Walt Disney World Resort, Epcot Center, and M.G.M. Studios.

Jährlich kommen Millionen von Leuten nach Orlando. Sie besuchen das Walt Disney Resort, das Epcot Center, die MGM Studios und natürlich das Zuhause von Mickey Mouse im Magic Kingdom.

Above right: Disney World Resort
Above left: MGM Studios
Right: Epcot Center
Opposite page top left and right: Cypress Gardens
Bottom: Universal Studios
Page 56: Sea World, Orlando

Todos los años millones de personas visitan Walt Disney World Resort, Epcot Center, y M.G.M. Studios.

All Pictures this page:

Chaque année des millions de personnes viennent la villégiature Walt Disney, Epcot Center et M
S

Im Cypress Gardens gibt es Unterhaltung von früh bis spät. Die Universal Studios in Florida bieten Ihnen die Möglichkeit, bei der Produktion von Film- und Fernsehaufnahmen dabeizusein.

91 Cypress Gardens

Cypress Gardens is an action-packed theme park. Universal Studios Florida production tours give visitors a behind-the-scene view into how movies and television shows are made.

Cypress Gardens es un parque de atracción con mucha acción. Los Paseos de Universal Studios les permite ver detrás de las escenas como las películas y shows de televisión se hacen.

Universal Studio

Les Cypress Gardens sont un parc thématique rempli d'activités. Des visites guidées par les Universal Studios montrent aux vacanciers ce qui se passe dans les coulisses et revèlent comment on fait des films et des spectacles de télévision.

Stuart
left: Jensen Beach
right: Fort Pierce

It was from Kennedy Space Center, that three astro[
blasted into space and landed on the Moon. Space[
U.S.A. is open to the public for tours of the facilities[

Von hier aus startete die Rakete auf ihrer Reise zum Mond. Der
weltbekannte Space Port U.S.A. ist für Besucher geöffnet.

Fue en Kennedy Space Center donde tres astronautas se lanzaron en
cohetes y llegaron a la luna. Space Port U.S.A. está abierto al público
para recorrer las instalaciones.

Above right: Kennedy Space Center,
Space Port USA
Above: Space Port USA
Right: Kennedy Space Center
Opposite page: Space Shuttle
lift off from Kennedy Space Center

Ce fut du Centre spatial Kennedy que
trois astronautes ont été propulsés dans
l'espace et ont aluni sur la Lune. Le
Spaceport U.S.A. est ouvert au public
qui peut faire des visites guidées des
installations.

Daytona Beach is famous for auto and motorcycles races. Visitors in cars can cruise directly on the sandy beaches.

Daytona Beach ist durch seine Auto- und Motoradrennen (Daytona 500) berühmt. Sie können mit Ihrem Auto direkt am Strand entlangfahren und die Sonne und das Meer genießen.

Top and bottom: Daytona B
Right page: Daytona Beach Pier at su

Daytona Beach es famosa por las carreras de autos y motocicletas. Los visitantes en sus carros pueden manejar directamente en las playas.

Daytona Beach est célèbre pour ses courses d'automobiles et de motocyclettes. Les visiteurs en voiture peuvent rouler lentement le long des plages de sable.

The oldest continuously occupied settlement in the United States is St. Aug
Founded by Pedro Menendez de Aviles in September 8, 1565; the city still refle
Spanish flavor. A visit to St. George Street and Spanish Quarter Living History Muse
a must. Guides, in authentic Spanish colonial costumes, take visitors through Am
early I

Die älteste Ansiedlung in Amerika ist St. Augustine, gegründet bei Pedro Mener
Aviles am 8. September des Jahres 1565. Noch heute ist der spanische Einfluß bem
Ein Besuch der St. George Straße und des restaurierten Viertels von ''St. Aug
Antigue'' zeigt Ihnen die Häuser und Bräuche der ersten amerikanischen Siedler.
''lebende'' Museum wird vom Staate Florida g

El pueblo más antiguo establecido y que continua ocupado en los Estados Unidos es St. Augustine. Fundado por Pedro Menéndez de Avilés en Septiembre 8 de 1565, la ciudad todavía refleja el sabor Español. Una visita a St. George Street y la Sección Española es un deber.

La ville la plus ancienne ayant été occupée continuellement aux Etats-Unis est St-Augustine. Fondée par Pedro Menéndez de Aviles le 8 septembre 1565, la ville dégage encore un parfum espagnol. Il faut aller voir la rue St-George et le musée d'histoire vivante du quartier espagnol. Des guides en costumes coloniaux espagnols authentiques conduisent les visiteurs à travers le début de l'histoire de l'Amérique.

Opposite page top right: Castillo de San Marco
Top left and middle: San Augustine Antiguo
Bottom: De Mesa Sanchez House
This page top: De Mesa Sanchez House
Bottom: St. Augustine Antiguo, restored area.
Following pages 66/67: Castillo de San Marco, St. Augustine

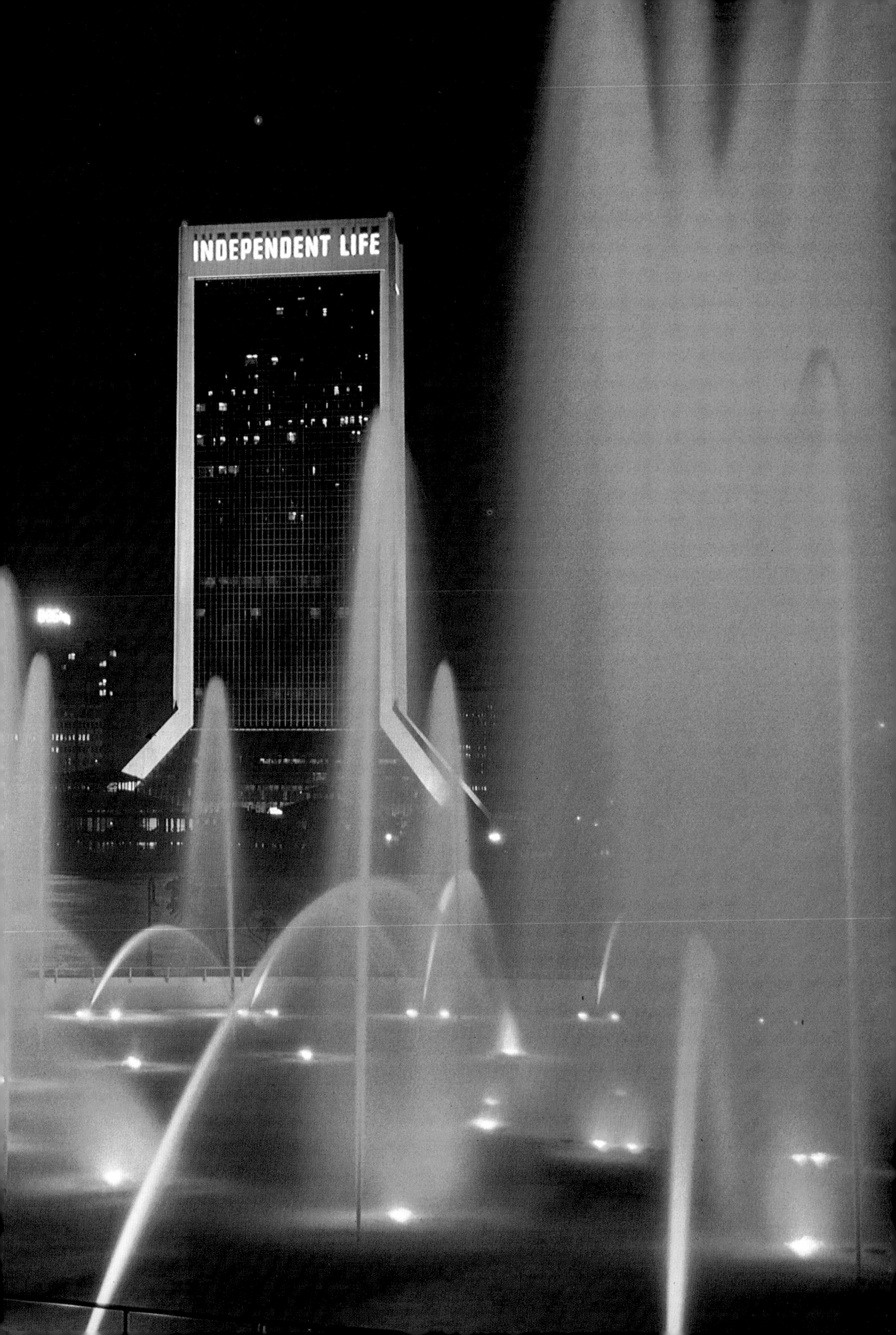
INDEPENDENT LIFE

Florida is one of the largest producers of citrus fruits in the world. Agriculture plays an important part in the economy of Florida.

Die Produktion von Zitrusfrüchten gehört für Florida zu den wichtigsten Einnhamequellen. Florida zählt zu den größten Produzenten von Orangen, Zitronen, etc.

La Florida es una de las más grandes productoras de frutas cítricas en el mundo. La agricultura es muy importante para la economía de la Florida.

La Floride est un des plus gros producteurs d'agrumes du monde. L'agriculture joue un rôle important dans l'économie de la Floride.

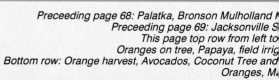

Preceeding page 68: Palatka, Bronson Mulholland
Preceeding page 69: Jacksonville S
This page top row from left to
Oranges on tree, Papaya, field irrig
Bottom row: Orange harvest, Avocados, Coconut Tree and
Oranges, M

70

Fernandina Beach on Amelia Island is famous for the shrimp industry. The beautiful restored Victorian Homes are open to the public as Bed and Breakfast Inns.

Fernardina Beach, auf der Insel Amelia, ist durch seine Shrimps-Erzeugung und wegen der schönen viktorianischen Häuser, heute häuptsachlich als Hotels betrieben, bekannt geworden.

Fernandina Beach en la Isla Amelia, es famosa por la industria de camarones. Las casas de tipo "Victorian" están abiertas al público como mesones.

Fernandina Beach dans l'île Amelia Island est célèbre pour la pêche à la crevette. Les magnifiques villas victoriennes restorées sont ouvertes au public comme auberges offrant le logement et le petit déjeuner.

Opposite page top: Fernadina Beach on Amelia Island
Middle: Catch of the day
Bottom: Pelican
This page top: Fort clinch on Amelia Island
Middle: Fernandina Bed and Breakfast Inn
Below: Fernandina fishing fleet
Following pages 74/75: Silver Springs

Opposite page top: Brooksville City Hall
Bottom: Crystal Springs
This page top: Weeki Wachee
Middle: Hibiscus flower
Bottom: Alligator

Silver Springs is one of the many fresh water springs in Florida, with a unique vegetation and marine-life. The glassbottom boats show the visitors the wonders below.
Tallahassee is the capital of Florida. Wakulla Springs is Florida's most impressive fresh water spring. Fossils of animals indicate life has existed here for millions of years.

Silver Springs ist eine der vielen Süßwasserquellen, mit einem mannigfaltigen Angebot im Bereich der Pflanzen- und Tierwelt. Das "Glasbodenboot" zeigt Ihnen die Einmaligkeit der Unterwasserwelt. Floridas Hauptstadt ist Talahassee. Wakulla Springs ist Floridas größte Süßwasserquelle. Diverse Funde bestätigen, daß hier schon vor Jahrhunderten Menschen gelebt haben müssen.

Silver Springs es uno de los muchos manantiales de agua en la Florida, con una vegetación y vida marítima única. El bote glassbottom enseña a los visitantes la maravilla del fondo del mar.
La Capital de la Florida es Tallahassee. El Manantial Wakulla es el más grande de la Florida. Fósiles de miles de años fueron descubiertos aquí.

Panorama on top: Wakulla Springs
Right: Cypress trees in Wakulla Springs
Opposite page, middle left: St. George Island
Bottom: Sunset in the Panhandle
Following page: Tallahassee State Capitol

Silver Springs est l'une de
nombreuses sources d'eau naturelle
de la Floride avec une végétation et
une vie marine uniques. Des bateaux
à fond de verre montrent aux
visiteurs les merveilles des
profondeurs.
Tallahassee est la capitale de la
Floride. Wakulla Springs est la
source d'eau naturelle la plus
impressionnante de la Floride.